MW01028769

Perseverance

A LONG OBEDIENCE
IN THE SAME DIRECTION

Eugene Peterson
with Dale & Sandy Larsen

6 STUDIES FOR INDIVIDUALS OR GROUPS
WITH LEADER'S NOTES

Inter-Varsity Press
Nottingham, England

IVP Connect
An imprint of InterVarsity Press
Downers Grove, Illinois

InterVarsity Press, USA
P.O. Box 1400, Downers Grove, IL 60515-1426, USA
World Wide Web: www.ivpress.com
Email: email@ivpress.com

Inter-Varsity Press, England
Norton Street, Nottingham NG7 3HR, England
World Wide Web: www.ivpbooks.com
Email: ivp@ivpbooks.com

InterVarsity Press®, U.S.A., is the book-publishing division of InterVarsity Christian Fellowship/USA®, a movement of students and faculty active on campus at hundreds of universities, colleges and schools of nursing in the United States of America, and a member movement of the International Fellowship of Evangelical Students. For information about local and regional activities, write Public Relations Dept., InterVarsity Christian Fellowship/USA, 6400 Schroeder Rd., P.O. Box 7895, Madison, WI 53707-7895, or visit the IVCF website at <www.intervarsity.org>.

This study guide is based on and adapts material from A Long Obedience in the Same Direction ©1980 by InterVarsity Christian Fellowship of the United States of America.

Inter-Varsity Press, England, is closely linked with the Universities and Colleges Christian Fellowship (formerly the Inter-Varsity Fellowship), a student movement linking Christian Unions in universities and colleges throughout the United Kingdom and the Republic of Ireland, and a member movement of the International Fellowship of Evangelical Students. For information about local and national activities write to UCCF, 38 De Montfort Street, Leicester LE1 7GP, email them at email@uccf.org.uk, or visit the UCCF website at www.uccf.org.uk.

Cover design: Cindy Kiple; cover photograph: Bartosz Hadyniak/iStockphoto

USA ISBN 978-0-8308-2010-8

UK ISBN 978-0-85111-379-1

Printed in the United States of America ∞

| P | 25 | 24 | 23 | 22 | 21 | 20 | 19 | 18 | 17 | 16 | 15 | 14 | 13 |
| Y | 24 | 23 | 22 | 21 | 20 | 19 | 18 | 17 | 16 | 15 | 14 | 13 | |

CONTENTS

Christian Basics Bible Studies

Knowing Christ is where faith begins. From there we grow through the essentials of discipleship: Bible study, prayer, Christian community and much more. We learn to set godly priorities, grow in Christian character and witness to others. We persevere through doubts and grow in wisdom. These are the topics woven into each of the Christian Basics Bible Studies. Working through this series will help you become a more mature Christian.

WHAT KIND OF GUIDE IS THIS?

The studies are not designed to merely tell you what one person thinks. Instead, through inductive study, they will help you discover for yourself what Scripture is saying. Each study deals with a particular passage—rather than jumping around the Bible—so that you can really delve into the author's meaning in that context.

The studies ask three different kinds of questions. *Observation* questions help you to understand the content of the passage by asking about the basic facts: who, what, when, where and how. *Interpretation* questions delve into the meaning of the passage. *Application* questions help you discover its implications for growing in Christ.

These three keys unlock the treasures of the biblical writings and help you live them out.

This is a thought-provoking guide. Each question assumes a variety of answers. Many questions do not have "right" answers, particularly questions that aim at meaning or application. Instead, the questions should inspire users to explore the passage more thoroughly.

This study guide is flexible. You can use it for individual study, but it is also great for a variety of groups—student, professional, neighborhood or church groups. Each study takes about forty-five minutes in a group setting or thirty minutes in personal study.

How They're Put Together

Each study is composed of four sections: opening paragraphs and questions to help you get into the topic, the NIV text and questions that invite study of the passage, questions to help you apply what you have learned, and a suggestion for prayer.

The workbook format provides space for writing a response to each question. This format is ideal for personal study and allows group members to prepare in advance for the discussion and/or write down notes during the study. This space can form a permanent record of your thoughts and spiritual progress.

At the back of the guide are study notes that may be useful for leaders or for individuals. These notes do not give "the answers," but they do provide additional background information on certain questions to help you through the difficult spots. The "Guidelines for Leaders" section describes how to lead a group discussion, gives helpful tips on group dynamics and suggests ways to deal with problems which may arise during the discussion. With such helps, someone with little or no experience can lead an effective group study.

SUGGESTIONS FOR INDIVIDUAL STUDY

1. This guide is based on a classic book or booklet that will enrich your spiritual life. If you have not read the book or booklet suggested in the "Further Reading" section, you may want to read the portion suggested before you begin your study. The ideas in the book will enhance your study, but the Bible text will be the focus of each session.

2. Read the introduction. Consider the opening questions and note your responses.

3. Pray, asking God to speak to you from his Word about this particular topic.

4. Read the passage reproduced for you from the New International Version. You may wish to mark phrases that seem important. Note in the margin any questions that come to your mind as you read.

5. Use the questions from the study guide to more thoroughly examine the passage. Note your findings in the space provided. After you have made your own notes, read the corresponding study notes in the back of the book for further insights.

6. Reread the entire passage, making further notes about its general principles and about the way you intend to use them.

7. Move to the "Commit" section. Spend time prayerfully considering what the passage has to say specifically to your life.

8. Read the suggestion for prayer. Speak to God about insights you have gained. Tell him of any desires you have for specific growth. Ask him to help you as you attempt to live out the principles described in that passage.

SUGGESTIONS FOR MEMBERS OF A GROUP STUDY

Joining a Bible study group can be a great avenue to spiritual growth. Here are a few guidelines that will help you as you participate in the studies in this guide.

1. Reading the book suggested as further reading, before or after each session, will enhance your study and understanding of the themes in this guide.

2. These studies focus on a particular passage of Scripture—in depth. Only rarely should you refer to other portions of the Bible, and then only at the request of the leader. Of course, the Bible is internally consistent. Other good forms of study draw on that consistency, but inductive Bible study sticks with a single passage and works on it in depth.

3. These are discussion studies. Questions in this guide aim at helping a group discuss together a passage of Scripture in order to understand its content, meaning and implications. Most people are either natural talkers or natural listeners, yet this type of study works best if people participate more or less evenly. Try to curb any natural tendency to either excessive talking or excessive quiet. You and the rest of the group will benefit.

4. Most questions in this guide allow for a variety of answers. If you disagree with someone else's comment, gently say so. Then explain your own point of view from the passage before you.

5. Be willing to lead a discussion, if asked. Much of the preparation for leading has already been accomplished in the writing of this guide.

6. Respect the privacy of people in your group. Many people speak

of things within the context of a Bible study/prayer group that they do not want to be public knowledge. Assume that personal information spoken within the group setting is private, unless you are specifically told otherwise. And don't talk about it elsewhere.

7. We recommend that all groups follow a few basic guidelines and that these guidelines be read at the first session. The guidelines, which you may wish to adapt to your situation, are the following:

   a. Anything said in this group is considered confidential and will not be discussed outside the group unless specific permission is given to do so.

   b. We will provide time for each person present to talk if he or she feels comfortable doing so.

   c. We will talk about ourselves and our own situations, avoiding conversation about other people.

   d. We will listen attentively to each other.

   e. We will pray for each other.

8. Enjoy your study. Prepare to grow.

SUGGESTIONS FOR GROUP LEADERS

There are specific suggestions to help you in leading in the "Guidelines for Leaders" and in the "Study Notes" at the back of this guide. Read the "Guidelines for Leaders" carefully, even if you are only leading one group meeting. Then you can go to the section on the particular session you will lead.

Tourists and Pilgrims

The essential thing "in heaven and earth" is . . . that there should be long obedience in the same direction; there thereby results, and has always resulted in the long run, something which has made life worth living. (Friedrich Nietzsche, Beyond Good and Evil)

This world is no friend to grace. A person who makes a commitment to Jesus Christ as Lord and Savior does not find a crowd immediately forming to applaud the decision nor old friends spontaneously gathering around to offer congratulations and counsel. Ordinarily there is nothing directly hostile, but an accumulation of puzzled disapproval and agnostic indifference constitutes, nevertheless, surprisingly formidable opposition.

It is nearly as hard for a sinner to recognize the world's temptations as it is for a fish to discover impurities in the water. There is a sense, a feeling, that things aren't right, that the environment is not whole, but just what it is eludes analysis. We know that the spiritual atmosphere in which we live erodes faith, dissipates hope and corrupts love, but it is hard to put our finger on what is wrong.

TOURISTS AND PILGRIMS

One aspect of *world* that I have been able to identify as harmful to Christians is the assumption that anything worthwhile can be acquired at once. We assume that if something can be done at all, it can be done quickly and efficiently. Our attention spans have been conditioned by thirty-second commercials. Our sense of reality has been flattened by thirty-page abridgments.

In our kind of culture anything, even news about God, can be sold if it is packaged freshly; but when it loses its novelty, it goes on the garbage heap. There is a great market for religious experience in our world; there is little enthusiasm for the patient acquisition of virtue, little inclination to sign up for a long apprenticeship in what earlier generations of Christians called holiness.

Everyone is in a hurry. The persons whom I lead in worship, among whom I counsel, visit, pray, preach and teach, want shortcuts. They want me to help them fill out the form that will get them instant credit (in eternity). They are impatient for results. They have adopted the lifestyle of a tourist and only want the high points. But a pastor is not a tour guide. I have no interest in telling apocryphal religious stories at and around dubiously identified sacred sites. The Christian life cannot mature under such conditions and in such ways.

A DOG-EARED SONGBOOK

In the pastoral work of training people in discipleship and accompanying them in pilgrimage, I have found, tucked away in the Hebrew Psalter, an old dog-eared songbook. I have used it to provide continuity in guiding others in the Christian way and directing people of faith in the conscious and continuous effort which develops into maturity in Christ. The songs are the psalms numbered 120 through 134 in the book of Psalms.

These fifteen psalms were likely sung, possibly in sequence, by Hebrew pilgrims as they went up to Jerusalem to the great worship festivals. Jerusalem was the highest city geographically in Palestine, and so all who traveled there spent much of their time ascending. But the ascent was not only literal, it was also metaphorical: the trip to Jerusalem acted out a life lived upward toward God, an existence that advanced from one level to another in developing maturity. What Paul described as "the upward call of God in Christ Jesus" (Philippians 3:14 RSV).

This picture of the Hebrews singing these fifteen psalms as they left their routines of discipleship and made their way from towns and villages, farms and cities, as pilgrims up to Jerusalem has become embedded in the Christian devotional imagination. It is our best background for understanding life as a faith journey. There are no better "songs for the road" for those who travel the way of faith in Christ.

For those who choose to live no longer as tourists, but as pilgrims, the Psalms of Ascents combine all the cheerfulness of a travel song with the practicality of a guidebook and map. Their unpretentious brevity is excellently described by William Faulkner: "They are not monuments, but footprints. A monument only says, 'At least I got this far,' while a footprint says, 'This is where I was when I moved again.' "

For further reading: chapter one of A Long Obedience in the Same Direction. (This guide builds on ideas outlined in A Long Obedience in the Same Direction. Recommended reading at the end of each study points you to the appropriate section of that book.)

Repentance

Psalm 120

My grandfather left Norway eighty years ago in the midst of a famine. His wife and ten children remained behind until he could return and get them. He came to Pittsburgh and worked in the steel mills for two years until he had enough money to go back and get his family. When he returned with them he didn't stay in Pittsburgh, although it had served his purposes well enough the first time, but he traveled on to Montana, plunging into new land, looking for a better place.

In all these immigrant stories there are mixed parts of escape and adventure: the escape from an unpleasant situation, and the adventure of a far better way of life, free for new things, open for growth and creativity. Every Christian has some variation on this immigrant plot to tell.

"Woe to me that I dwell in Meshech, that I live among the tents of Kedar! Too long have I lived among those who hate peace." This is the text of Psalm 120. But we don't have to live there any longer. Repentance, the first word in Christian immigration, sets us on the way to traveling in the light. It is a rejection that is also an acceptance, a leaving that develops into an arriving, a no to the world that is a yes to God.

OPEN

■ What aspects of your own world do you find distressing or unsatisfying?

__ my community   __ violence   __ lack of commitment

__ dishonesty   __ sources of entertainment

__ frantic pace   __ lack of purpose   __ the government

■ What motivates you to turn away from sin and move toward greater closeness with God?

__ promise of blessing   __ desire to set an example for others

__ curiosity about who God is   __ desire to know God better

__ past experience with the Lord   __other:_____

STUDY

Read Psalm 120.

[1]I call on the LORD in my distress,
    and he answers me.
[2]Save me, O LORD, from lying lips
    and from deceitful tongues.

[3]What will he do to you,
    and what more besides, O deceitful tongue?
[4]He will punish you with a warrior's sharp arrows,
    with burning coals of the broom tree.

[5]Woe to me that I dwell in Meshech,

that I live among the tents of Kedar!

⁶Too long have I lived
among those who hate peace.

⁷I am a man of peace;
but when I speak, they are for war.

---

1. Throughout this passage, what words and phrases reveal how the writer feels about his society?

---

2. As the psalmist begins the ascent toward God's temple in Jerusalem, what does he feel distressed about (vv. 1-2)?

---

3. What does he ask the Lord to do for him in his distress?

---

4. Note the strong imagery of the punishments in verse 4. Why do you think the deceitful tongue deserves such harsh punishment?

5. How are your own feelings about sin like or unlike what the psalmist expresses?

6. How does the sin the psalmist identifies in verses 6-7 compare or contrast with the sin in verses 1-2?

7. Sometimes sins that are rooted deep in our culture are difficult to identify—and may take root in us! How has this been true for you?

8. How does the psalmist think and act decisively about sin?

COMMIT

■ What undesirable elements in your environment do you need to move away from—without breaking godly commitments?

How can you take that step?

■ While we cannot always move away from worldliness, we can always repent and abandon it in our hearts. What sin do you need to confess and forsake?

Take the step of moving away from the world and toward God. Begin— or renew—your commitment to be a pilgrim.

For further reading: *chapter two of* A Long Obedience in the Same Direction.

Help
Psalm 124

I was at a Red Cross bloodmobile to donate my annual pint and was being asked a series of questions by a nurse to see if there was any reason for disqualification. The final question on the list was, "Do you engage in hazardous work?" I said, "Yes."

She was interrupted from her routine and looked up, a little surprised, for I was wearing a clerical collar by which she could identify me as a pastor. Her hesitation was only momentary; she smiled, ignored my answer and marked the no on her questionnaire, saying, "I don't mean *that* kind of hazardous."

I would like to have continued the conversation, comparing what she supposed I meant by hazardous with what I did in fact mean by it. But that was not the appropriate time and place. There was a line of people waiting for their turn at the needle. There are, though, appropriate times and places for just such conversations, and one of them is when Christians encounter Psalm 124. Psalm 124 is a song of hazard—and of help. Among the Psalms of Ascents sung by the people of God on the way of faith, this is one which, better than any other, describes the hazardous work of all discipleship and declares the help which is always experienced at the hand of God.

OPEN

- When have you survived danger (either physical or spiritual) through the Lord's help?

- In what ways do you feel the Lord has not helped or rescued you?

What do you wish God would do in those cases?

STUDY

Read Psalm 124.
¹If the LORD had not been on our side—
   let Israel say—
²if the LORD had not been on our side
   when men attacked us,
³when their anger flared against us,
   they would have swallowed us alive;
⁴the flood would have engulfed us,
   the torrent would have swept over us,
⁵the raging waters
   would have swept us away.

⁶Praise be to the LORD,
   who has not let us be torn by their teeth.

⁷We have escaped like a bird
       out of the fowler's snare;
the snare has been broken,
       and we have escaped.
⁸Our help is in the name of the LORD,
       the Maker of heaven and earth.

---

1. The psalmist, and not only the psalmist but all God's people, had been under vicious attack. What words depict the strength of the attack they had to endure?

---

2. What would have been their destiny if God had not rescued them (vv. 3-6)?

---

3. Gnashing teeth, raging floods and treacherous snares were part of the psalmist's reality. How are they part of the reality you are facing now? (They may take the form of persecutions, temptations, physical problems, conflicts or anything else that threatens your faith.)

4. To what does the psalmist compare their escape (v. 7)?

_____

5. When and how has the Lord helped you persevere in dangerous times?

_____

6. How does your history with the Lord give you hope that he will deliver you safely through danger?

_____

7. The last verse of the psalm proclaims that "Our help is in the name of the LORD, the Maker of heaven and earth." How is your trust in God affected by the knowledge that he is the Creator of all?

COMMIT

- What hazard or attack frightens you the most right now?

Why is it particularly frightening?

- What does it mean for you to know the Lord is on your side in this situation (vv. 1-2)?

Admit your fears to the Lord and ask him for his peace as you trust him for deliverance. Thank God for the stories of deliverance in the Scriptures, in others' lives and in your own life. Put your present and future in his hands.

For further reading: *chapter six of* A Long Obedience in the Same Direction.

Joy
Psalm 126

I know there are Christians, so-called, who never crack a smile and who can't abide a joke. But I don't meet very many of them. The stereotype of the somber Christian is a lie created, presumably, by the devil. One of the delightful discoveries along the way of Christian discipleship is how much enjoyment there is, how much laughter you hear, how much sheer fun you find.

Joy is characteristic of the Christian pilgrimage. It is the second in Paul's list of the fruits of the Spirit (Galatians 5:22). It is the first of Jesus' signs in the Gospel of John (turning water into wine).

Joy is not what we have to acquire in order to experience life in Christ; it is what comes to us when we are walking in the way of faith and obedience. We come to God (and to the revelation of God's ways) because none of us have it within ourselves, except momentarily, to be joyous. Joy cannot be commanded, purchased or arranged. But there is something we can do. We can decide to live in response to the abundance of God, and not under the dictatorship of our own poor needs. One of the certain consequences of such a life is joy, the kind expressed in Psalm 126.

 OPEN

■ How do you recognize a joyful person?

■ For you, what is the most joyful part of being a Christian?

 STUDY

Read Psalm 126.
¹When the LORD brought back the captives to Zion,
    we were like men who dreamed.
²Our mouths were filled with laughter,
    our tongues with songs of joy.
Then it was said among the nations,
    "The LORD has done great things for them."
³The LORD has done great things for us,
    and we are filled with joy.

⁴Restore our fortunes, O LORD,
    like streams in the Negev.
⁵Those who sow in tears
    will reap with songs of joy.
⁶He who goes out weeping,
    carrying seed to sow,
will return with songs of joy,
    carrying sheaves with him.

---

1. When they finally return from captivity in Babylon, how do God's people react?

2. Imagine the scene: crowds of Jewish exiles returning from distant, pagan Babylon to their home city of Jerusalem. What do you see and hear?

3. How does their joy strengthen the Lord's reputation among the Gentiles?

4. When has someone's joy in the Lord's work been an encouragement to you to keep going?

5. For the psalmist, the return to Zion is a glorious memory in a time of current trouble (v. 4). How do good memories increase your joy even in sorrowful times?

6. What promises does the psalm conclude with?

---

7. Weeping while sowing seed for the future is a powerful image of persevering in tough times. What "seeds" can you sow even in sorrow or dryness?

 COMMIT

- Reflect on times you have been able to say with the psalmist, "The LORD has done great things for us, and we are filled with joy." How can you keep those times fresher in your memory?

- In the light of past joys, we can continue to trust God even in dry times. How will you express your joyful trust in him today?

Express your joy in the Lord in some verbal or tangible way. Trust him that, no matter what happens, joy lies ahead for you.

For further reading: *chapter eight of* A Long Obedience in the Same Direction.

Patience

Psalm 129

Stick-to-it-iveness is one of the more inelegant words in the language, but I have a special fondness for it nevertheless. I heard the word a great deal when I was young, mostly, as I recall, from my mother.

I was a creature of sudden but short-lived enthusiasms. I had a passion for building model airplanes, and then one day, mysteriously, all desire left, and the basement was littered with half-finished models. Then stamp collecting became an all-consuming hobby. I received an immense stamp album for Christmas, joined a philatelic club, acquired piles and piles of stamps and then one day, unaccountably, the interest left me. The album gathered dust, and the mounds of stamps were left unmounted. Next it was horses. Each Saturday morning my best friend and I would ride our bikes to a dude ranch two miles from town, get horses and ride up into the Montana foothills, imagining we were Meriweather Lewis and William Clark, or, less pretentiously, Gene Autry and the Lone Ranger. And then, overnight, that entire world vanished and in its place was—girls.

After praising the many good effects of patience, Paul Goodman said, "But the patient person . . . does not enjoy it." I have also found that it is one of the marks of Christian discipleship and have learned to admire those who exemplify it. Along the way Psalm 129 has gotten included in my admiration.

OPEN

- I get impatient when_____

  _____.

- For me, patience is:

  __ easy   __ impossible

  __ it depends on what I have to be patient about

  __ other: _____

- Who is the most patient person you know? Describe some evidence of that person's patience.

STUDY

Read Psalm 129.

[1]They have greatly oppressed me from my youth—
   let Israel say—
[2]they have greatly oppressed me from my youth,
   but they have not gained the victory over me.
[3]Plowmen have plowed my back
   and made their furrows long.
[4]But the LORD is righteous;
   he has cut me free from the cords of the wicked.

[5]May all who hate Zion
   be turned back in shame.

⁶May they be like grass on the roof,
    which withers before it can grow;
⁷with it the reaper cannot fill his hands,
    nor the one who gathers fill his arms.
⁸May those who pass by not say,
    "The blessing of the LORD be upon you;
    we bless you in the name of the LORD."

---

1. As the psalmist looks back on his nation's history, what consistent pattern does he see?

---

2. Why has God intervened in attacks on Israel?

---

3. If you had written this psalm, who or what would "they" be in verses 1-2?

4. There is no sign in this psalm that Israel did anything to be deliv-
   ered—except wait. What would you say that waiting teaches the
   psalmist about himself?

5. What does waiting teach him about God?

6. What has waiting taught you about God?

7. What is the writer's wish for the destiny of God's enemies?

8. How does the writer express patience even in his wish for the
   destiny of God's enemies?

COMMIT

- When has the Lord enabled you to remain patient under attack?

- What are some long-term "oppressions" in your life in which you need patience for victory (as in vv. 1-2)?

Remember that patience is never enjoyable at the moment. Thank God for past and future victories, and ask him for the continual grace of patience.

For further reading: *chapter eleven of* A Long Obedience in the Same Direction.

STUDY FIVE

Hope
Psalm 130

I was once a watchman. I worked from 10:00 p.m. until 6:00 a.m. in a building in New York City. My work as a night watchman was combined with that of elevator operator, but the elevator work petered out about midnight. After that I sat and read, dozed or studied.

There were assorted night people in the neighborhood who would stop in and visit with me: strange, bizarre people with wonderful stories. I will never know how much of what I heard from them was fact and how much fiction: a failed millionaire obsessed with communist plots responsible for his demise, a South American adventurer now too old to tramp the remote jungles and mountains, a couple of streetwalkers who on slow nights would sit and talk about God and the worth of their souls.

The people who employed me thought it was worth several dollars an hour for me to wait through the night and watch for the morning. But I never did anything, never constructed anything, never made anything happen. I waited.

If I had not known that there were others in charge of the building, I might not have been content to just be a watchman and collect my pay. If I were not confident that the building had an owner who cared about it, if I did not know that there was a building engineer who kept it in good order and repair, if I did not know that there were hundreds of people in the building who were going about their work every day quite capably . . . if I had not known these things, I might not have been so relaxed in making idle gossip with women of the night and old men of storied pasts.

Nor would the psalmist have been content to be a watchman if he were not sure of God. The psalmist's and the Christian's waiting and hoping are based on the conviction that God is actively involved in his creation and vigorously at work in redemption.

 OPEN

- Reflect on a time when the Lord fulfilled your hopes. How did the experience strengthen your relationship with him?

- How did the actual events compare to your expectations of how and when your hopes would be fulfilled?

 STUDY

Read Psalm 130.
¹Out of the depths I cry to you, O LORD;
²O Lord, hear my voice.

Let your ears be attentive
  to my cry for mercy.

[3]If you, O LORD, kept a record of sins,
  O Lord, who could stand?
[4]But with you there is forgiveness;
  therefore you are feared.

[5]I wait for the LORD, my soul waits,
  and in his word I put my hope.
[6]My soul waits for the Lord
  more than watchmen wait for the morning,
  more than watchmen wait for the morning.

[7]O Israel, put your hope in the LORD,
  for with the LORD is unfailing love
  and with him is full redemption.
[8]He himself will redeem Israel
  from all their sins.

---

1. What insight does this passage give to the psalmist's relationship to the Lord?

---

2. The psalmist is obviously in deep trouble or distress of some kind.

What keeps his situation from being hopeless?

_____

3. How does God's mercy inspire hope (vv. 3-4, 7)?

_____

4. What reasons does the writer give Israel for putting their hope in the Lord?

_____

5. What are some false (worldly) hopes that people have?

_____

6. Throughout this psalm, the character of God inspires the psalmist's hope. What is it about God's character that maintains your hope?

7. For what are you waiting and watching in your spiritual life?

 COMMIT

- In what "depths" (perhaps as a result of your experience of waiting) do you now find yourself?

- How might worldly hopes be holding you in the depths?

- What part can God's forgiveness play in reaching into those depths?

Praise God for being Lord of your future. Ask him to cleanse you of false worldly hopes and help you rest your hope solely in him.

For further reading: *chapter twelve of* A Long Obedience in the Same Direction.

Faith

Psalm 132

The most religious places in the world are not churches but battlefields and mental hospitals. You are much more likely to find passionate prayer in a foxhole than in a church pew, and you will certainly find more otherworldly visions and supernatural voices in a mental hospital than you will in a church.

Nevertheless, we Christians don't go to either place to nurture our faith. We don't deliberately put ourselves in places of fearful danger to evoke heartfelt prayer, and we don't put ourselves in psychiatric wards so we can be around those who clearly see visions of heaven and hell and distinctly hear the voice of God. What most Christians do is come to church, a place that is fairly safe and moderately predictable. We have an instinct for health and sanity in our faith.

In doing that we don't get what some people seem to want very much, namely, a religion that makes us safe at all costs, certifying us as inoffensive to our neighbors and guaranteeing us as good credit risks to the banks. It would be simply awful to find that as we grew in Christ we became dull, that as we developed in discipleship we became like Anthony Trollope's Miss Thorne, whose "virtues were too numerous to describe, and not sufficiently interesting to deserve description."

We want a Christian faith that has stability but is not petrified; that has vision but is not hallucinatory. How do we get both the sense of stability and the spirit of adventure, the ballast of good health and the zest of true sanity? How do we get the adult maturity to keep our feet on the ground and retain the childlike innocence to make the leap of faith? Psalm 132 shows obedience as a lively, adventurous response of faith rooted in historical fact and reaching into a promised hope.

OPEN

- If I were to rate the purposes that drive my life, faith in the Lord would come:

  ___ first

  ___ somewhere below the following concerns: _____

  ___ lower than I'd like

  ___ it depends on the area of obedience

  ___ it depends on when you ask me

- For me putting faith in God is:

  ___ a chore   ___ a joy   ___ a struggle   ___ an opportunity

  Explain your responses.

- When is faith most real for you?

STUDY

Read Psalm 132.

[1]O LORD, remember David
　　and all the hardships he endured.
[2]He swore an oath to the LORD
　　and made a vow to the Mighty One of Jacob:
[3]"I will not enter my house
　　or go to my bed—
[4]I will allow no sleep to my eyes,
　　no slumber to my eyelids,
[5]till I find a place for the LORD,
　　a dwelling for the Mighty One of Jacob."

[6]We heard it in Ephrathah,
　　we came upon it in the fields of Jaar:
[7]"Let us go to his dwelling place;
　　let us worship at his footstool—
[8]arise, O LORD, and come to your resting place,
　　you and the ark of your might.
[9]May your priests be clothed with righteousness;
　　may your saints sing for joy."

[10]For the sake of David your servant,
　　do not reject your anointed one.

[11]The LORD swore an oath to David,
　　a sure oath that he will not revoke:
"One of your own descendants
　　I will place on your throne—

¹²if your sons keep my covenant
>   and the statutes I teach them,
> then their sons will sit
>   on your throne for ever and ever."

¹³For the LORD has chosen Zion,
>   he has desired it for his dwelling:
¹⁴"This is my resting place for ever and ever;
>   here I will sit enthroned, for I have desired it—
¹⁵I will bless her with abundant provisions;
>   her poor will I satisfy with food.
¹⁶I will clothe her priests with salvation,
>   and her saints will ever sing for joy.

¹⁷Here I will make a horn grow for David
>   and set up a lamp for my anointed one.
¹⁸I will clothe his enemies with shame,
>   but the crown on his head will be resplendent."

---

1. What words and phrases indicate how David feels about God?

---

2. What consuming purpose is David pursuing (vv. 2-5)?

3. What was the mood when the ark of the covenant was finally brought to Jerusalem (vv. 7-9)?

4. This passage gives us a sense of David's joy in persistently following God. What keeps you persisting in your faith?

5. How did the Lord assure Israel of future blessings (vv. 11-18)?

6. How does the faithfulness of others (past or present) inspire you to persevere in obeying God?

7. How does the assurance of God's faithfulness encourage you to obey him?

8. How would you describe the relationship between faith and obedience?

 COMMIT

- Obedience to God can be strengthened in any area: where we are now actively disobeying, where we are now just indifferent, or where we are now obeying God but half-heartedly or only outwardly. Where would you like to strengthen your obedience to the Lord?

- How will you bring those parts of your life into closer harmony with God's will?

Thank God for the rewards and blessings that have come into your life through obeying him. Thank him also for the people whose obedience serves as a living example for you. Confess any disobedience, and commit yourself to following him.

For further reading: *chapter fourteen of* A Long Obedience in the Same Direction.

GUIDELINES FOR LEADERS

Leading a Bible discussion can be an enjoyable and rewarding experience. But it can also be intimidating—especially if you've never done it before. If this is how you feel, you're in good company. Remember when God asked Moses to lead the Israelites out of Egypt? Moses replied, "O Lord, please send someone else to do it" (Ex 4:13). But God gave Moses the help (human and divine) he needed to be a strong leader.

Leading a Bible discussion is not difficult if you follow certain guidelines. You don't need to be an expert on the Bible or a trained teacher. The suggestions listed below can help you to effectively fulfill your role as leader—and enjoy doing it.

PREPARING FOR THE STUDY

1. As you study the passage ahead of time, ask God to help you understand it and apply it in your own life. Unless this happens, you will not be prepared to lead others. Pray too for the various members of the group. Ask God to open your hearts to the message of his Word and motivate you to action.

2. Read the introduction to the entire guide to get an overview of the subject at hand and the issues that will be explored.

3. Be ready for the "Open" questions with a personal story or example. The group will be only as vulnerable and open as its leader.

4. Read the chapter of the companion book that is suggested under "Further Reading" at the end of each study.

5. As you begin preparing for each study, read and reread the assigned Bible passage to familiarize yourself with it. You may want to look up the passage in a Bible so that you can see its context.

6. This study guide is based on the New International Version of the Bible. That is what is reproduced in your guide. It will help you and the group if you use this translation as the basis for your study and discussion.

7. Carefully work through each question in the study. Spend time in meditation and reflection as you consider how to respond.

8. Write your thoughts and responses in the space provided in the study guide. This will help you to express your understanding of the passage clearly.

9. It might help you to have a Bible dictionary handy. Use it to look up any unfamiliar words, names or places.

10. Take the final (application) questions and the "Commit" portion of each study seriously. Consider what this means for your life, what changes you may need to make in your lifestyle and/or what actions you can take in your church or with people you know. Remember that the group will follow your lead in responding to the studies.

LEADING THE STUDY

1. Be sure everyone in your group has a study guide and Bible. Encourage the group to prepare beforehand for each discussion by

reading the introduction to the guide and by working through the questions in the study.

2. At the beginning of your first time together, explain that these studies are meant to be discussions, not lectures. Encourage the members of the group to participate. However, do not put pressure on those who may be hesitant to speak during the first few sessions.

3. Begin the study on time. Open with prayer, asking God to help the group understand and apply the passage.

4. Have a group member read the introductory paragraph at the beginning of the discussion. This will remind the group of the topic of the study.

5. Every study begins with a section called "Open." These "approach" questions are meant to be asked before the passage is read. They are important for several reasons.

First, there is always a stiffness that needs to be overcome before people will begin to talk openly. A good question will break the ice.

Second, most people will have lots of different things going on in their minds (dinner, an exam, an important meeting coming up, how to get the car fixed) that have nothing to do with the study. A creative question will get their attention and draw them into the discussion.

Third, approach questions can reveal where our thoughts or feelings need to be transformed by Scripture. That is why it is especially important not to read the passage before the approach question is asked. The passage will tend to color the honest reactions people would otherwise give, because they feel they are supposed to think the way the Bible does.

6. Have a group member read aloud the passage to be studied.

7. As you ask the questions, keep in mind that they are designed to be used just as they are written. You may simply read them aloud. Or you may prefer to express them in your own words.

   There may be times when it is appropriate to deviate from the study guide. For example, a question may already have been answered. If so, move on to the next question. Or someone may raise an important question not covered in the guide. Take time to discuss it, but try to keep the group from going off on tangents.

8. Avoid answering your own questions. Repeat or rephrase them if necessary until they are clearly understood. An eager group quickly becomes passive and silent if members think the leader will give all the *right* answers.

9. Don't be afraid of silence. People may need time to think about the question before formulating their answers.

10. Don't be content with just one answer. Ask, "What do the rest of you think?" or, "Anything else?" until several people have given answers to a question.

11. Acknowledge all contributions. Be affirming whenever possible. Never reject an answer. If it is clearly off-base, ask, "Which verse led you to that conclusion?" or, "What do the rest of you think?"

12. Don't expect every answer to be addressed to you, even though this will probably happen at first. As group members become more at ease, they will begin to truly interact with each other. This is one sign of healthy discussion.

13. Don't be afraid of controversy. It can be stimulating! If you don't resolve an issue completely, don't be frustrated. Move on and keep it in mind for later. A subsequent study may solve the problem.

14. Periodically summarize what the group has said about the passage. This helps to draw together the various ideas mentioned and gives continuity to the study. But don't preach.

15. Don't skip over the application questions at the end of each study. It's important that we each apply the message of the passage to ourselves in a specific way. Be willing to get things started by describing how you have been affected by the study.

    Depending on the makeup of your group and the length of time you've been together, you may or may not want to discuss the "Commit" section. If not, allow the group to read it and reflect on it silently. Encourage members to make specific commitments and to write them in their study guide. Ask them the following week how they did with their commitments.

16. Conclude your time together with conversational prayer. Ask for God's help in following through on the commitments you've made.

17. End on time.

Many more suggestions and helps are found in The Big Book on Small Groups *by Jeffrey Arnold.*

Study One. REPENTANCE. Psalm 120.

Purpose: To encourage us to turn away from sin and toward the Lord.

Question 2.

Notice in particular that he asks the Lord to answer him (v. 1), save him (v. 2) and punish sinners (v. 4).

Question 3.

"The psalms are full of references to the sins of the tongue—lies, scandal, slander, hypocrisy." People of God "may suffer as much from what people say as from what they do" (David Alexander and Pat Alexander, eds., *Eerdmans' Handbook to the Bible* [Grand Rapids, Mich.: Eerdmans, 1973], p. 350).

Question 7.

It is good to remember that the "deceitful tongue" of verse 3 could be the writer's own—or ours! We are called to reject sin no matter where we find it, in others or in ourselves.

Question 8.

The first step toward God is a step away from the lies of the world. It is a renunciation of the lies we have been told about ourselves and our neighbors and our universe. Repentance is not an emotion. It is not feeling sorry for your sins. It is a decision. It is deciding you have been wrong in supposing that you could manage your own life and be your own god; it is deciding that you were wrong in thinking that you had, or could get, the strength, education and training to make it on your own.

Study Two.   HELP. Psalm 124.

Purpose: To praise God for his help in the past and trust him for future deliverance.

General note.

Statements like "God is on our side" and "God is our help" are red flags for some. They provoke challenges. People say, "The Lord might be on *your* side, he might be *your* help, but he is not *mine.*" Be aware of these feelings in others, but don't allow yourself to be forced into the position of being God's defender—explaining God to his disappointed clients. God doesn't need us to defend him. Let this psalm do its work in pointing us to a better understanding of God.

Question 1.

The people were in danger of being swallowed up alive and drowned by flood. The first picture is of an enormous dragon or sea monster. The second picture, that of a flood, is a picture of sudden disaster. In the Middle East, watercourses that have eroded the countryside are all interconnected by an intricate, gravitational system. A sudden storm fills the little gullies with water, they feed into one another, and in a few minutes a torrential flash flood is produced. Persons who live in these desert areas are endangered during the rainy season by such unannounced catastrophes.

Question 2.

The psalmist is not talking about the good life, how God has kept him out of all difficulty. This person has gone through the worst—the dragon's mouth, the flood's torrent—and finds himself intact. He was not abandoned but helped. The final strength is not in the dragon or in the flood but in "the LORD who was on our side."

Question 4.

The simile of danger changes from floodwaters to "the fowler's snare," which also occurs in Psalm 91:3. This bird trap "consisted of a roughly circular wooden base on which two nets were mounted. When the trap was set, the nets were drawn down to one side and held in place by a trigger, which, when released, allowed the nets to spring up and envelop the victim. The trigger could be released by hand, or sprung when the victim touched the bait attached to it" (L. E. Toombs, "Traps and Snares," in *The Interpreter's Dictionary of the Bible*, ed. George Arthur Buttrick [Nashville: Abingdon, 1962], p. 688).

Study Three. JOY. Psalm 126.

> *Purpose:* To rejoice in what God has done, is doing and will do for us.

General note.

The Babylonian king Nebuchadnezzar besieged Jerusalem for years and eventually conquered it in 586 B.C. The city and temple were broken down and ransacked, many of the Jews killed, and most of the survivors taken into exile in Babylon. (See 2 Kings 24—25 and 2 Chron 36.) After the Persians took over the kingdom of the Babylonians, King Cyrus allowed the Jews to return and rebuild their city and temple (as related in the books of Nehemiah and Ezra). Psalm 126 celebrates the return of the exiles from the Babylonian captivity.

Question 1.

The central sentence in the psalm is "We are glad," or "We are filled with joy" (v. 3). The words on one side of that center (vv. 1-2) are in the past tense, the words on the other side (vv. 4-6) in the future tense. Present gladness has past and future. It is not a spurt of good feelings that comes when the weather and the stock market are both right on the same day.

Question 6.

The Negev is the long southern triangle of modern Israel, still known by that name today. Its watercourses would be dry much of the year and then flood with seasonal rain. Farmers carried their seed out to the field and scattered it by hand, a laborious process. Verse 6 is, of course, the inspiration for the missionary hymn "Bringing In the Sheaves" (by George A. Minor and Knowles Shaw).

Study Four.   PATIENCE. Psalm 129.

Purpose: To see patience not as passivity but as a positive force for good. And to learn to wait for the Lord with patience.

Question 1.

Note in verses 3-4 that the harness cords, connecting plow to oxen, have been severed. The plows of persecution aren't working, and the oxherds haven't even noticed! They plod back and forth, unaware that their opposition is worthless. If they ever looked behind them (which they never do—their stiff necks make that exercise too painful), they would see that their bluster and blasphemy are having no results at all.

Question 2.

Not because the psalmist and his people are deserving but because "the LORD is righteous" (v. 4).

Question 4.

Verses 1-3 describe the psalmist's suffering. He has discovered his own endurance in the midst of oppression, as his enemies have not been victorious over him.

Question 7.

Palestinian houses were flat-topped; dirt was spread on the roofs for insulation. Seeds would sprout and grow from this dirt, but the grass didn't last; the thin soil couldn't support it. By midday the grass withered. No harvest there. The illustration is a cartoon, designed to bring a smile to the people of faith. The life of the world that is opposed or indifferent to God is barren and futile.

> The psalmists are realistic in recognizing that right *cannot* triumph without the actual overthrow of evil and punishment of wrong. We pray "Thy kingdom come." But we are often horrified when the psalmists spell out what this means—perhaps because we are less in

love with good, less opposed to evil than they were; or because many of us have never known real persecution for our faith; or because we value life more than right. (*Eerdmans' Handbook*, p. 339)

Study Five.   HOPE. Psalm 130.

Purpose: *To focus on God as our great hope.*

Question 2.

Note how each verse of the psalm includes a positive statement about the Lord.

Question 3.

The mercy of God spells hope for us only after we have realized that our situation without God's mercy is hopeless (v. 3).

Question 5.

There are many possibilities: unshakable financial security, health and fitness into old age, status, longevity, power in relationships. These things bring benefits, but they are not guaranteed to be there when we need them.

Question 6.

Eight times the name of God is used in the psalm. We find, as we observe how God is addressed, that he is understood as one who forgives sin, who comes to those who wait and hope in him, who is characterized by steadfast love and plenteous redemption, and who will redeem Israel. God makes a difference. He acts positively toward his people.

Study Six.   FAITH. Psalm 132.

> **Purpose:** To make us more sensitive to areas where we
> should deepen our faith in and obedience to the Lord.

Questions 2-3.

The Philistines had captured the ark of the covenant years earlier.
When David became king, he defeated the Philistines. News had
come to David of where the ark was; he vowed to get it and said: "Let
us go to his dwelling place; let us worship at his footstool." He went
to the ark and brought it up to Jerusalem in festive parade: "Arise,
O LORD, and come to your resting place, you and the ark of your
might. May your priests be clothed with righteousness; may your
saints sing for joy." As the song was sung we are told that "David . . .
danced before the LORD with all his might, while he and the entire
house of Israel brought up the ark of the LORD with shouts and the
sound of trumpets" (2 Sam 6:14-15).

Question 4.

We should not be intimidated by David in this passage. David's own
story includes many ups and downs in following God. Still, we see
here that the times of strong obedience brought him great joy.

Question 6.

Think of specific people whose obedience to the Lord has been an
example to you. You might include biblical people, well-known
Christians, unsung heroes you have heard of, personal acquaintan-
ces or family members.

Christian Basics are the keys to becoming a mature disciple. The studies in these guides, based on material from some well-loved books (which can be read along with the studies), will take you through key Scripture passages and help you to apply biblical truths to your life. Each guide has six studies for individuals or groups.

CERTAINTY: *Know Why You Believe*
Paul Little
Faith means facing hard questions. Is Jesus the only way to God? Why does God allow suffering and evil? These questions need solid answers. These studies will guide you to Scripture to find a reasonable response to the toughest challenges you face.

CHARACTER: *Who You Are When No One's Looking*
Bill Hybels
Courage. Discipline. Vision. Endurance. Compassion. Self-sacrifice. The qualities covered in this Bible study guide provide a foundation for character. With this foundation and God's guidance, we can maintain character even when we face temptations and troubles.

CHRIST: *Basic Christianity*
John Stott
God himself is seeking us through his Son, Jesus Christ. But who is

this Jesus? These studies explore the person and character of the man who has altered the face of history. Discover him for the first time or in a new and deeper way.

COMMITMENT: *My Heart—Christ's Home*
Robert Boyd Munger

What would it be like to have Christ come into the home of our hearts? Moving from the living room to the study to the recreation room with him, we discover what he desires for us. These studies will take you through six rooms of your heart. You will be stretched and enriched by your personal meetings with Christ in each study.

DECISIONS: *Finding God's Will*
J. I. Packer

Facing a big decision? From job changes to marriage to buying a house, this guide will give you the biblical grounding you need to discover what God has in store for you.

EXCELLENCE: *Run with the Horses*
Eugene Peterson

Life is difficult. Daily we must choose whether to live cautiously or courageously. God calls us to live at our best, to pursue righteousness, to sustain a drive toward excellence. These studies on Jeremiah's pursuit of excellence with God's help will motivate and inspire you.

HOPE: *Never Beyond Hope*
J. I. Packer and Carolyn Nystrom

Ever feel like a hopeless sinner? Look at the lives of Samson, Peter, Martha and more. The Bible was given to us to offer hope and encouragement through the testimonies of those that have gone before us. Through this guide, you'll discover that just as biblical characters failed, biblical characters were redeemed. And God wants to do the same for you.

PERSEVERANCE: *A Long Obedience in the Same Direction*
Eugene Peterson

When the going gets tough, what does a Christian do? This world is no friend to grace. God has given us some resources, however. As we grow in character qualities like hope, patience, repentance and joy, we will grow in our ability to persevere. The biblical passages in these studies offer encouragement to continue in the path Christ has set forth for us.

PRAYER: *Too Busy Not to Pray*
Bill Hybels

There's so much going on—work, church, school, family, relationships: the list is never-ending. Someone always seems to need something from us. But time for God, time to pray, seems impossible to find. These studies are designed to help you slow down and listen to God so that you can respond to him.

PRIORITIES: *Tyranny of the Urgent*
Charles Hummel

Have you ever wished for a thirty-hour day? Every week we leave a trail of unfinished tasks. Unanswered letters, unvisited friends and unread books haunt our waking moments. We desperately need relief. This guide is designed to help you put your life back in order by discovering what is *really* important. Find out what God's priorities are for you.

TRANSFORMATION: *Developing a Heart for God*
Rebecca Manley Pippert
Would you like to move from despair to hope? Would you like to transform your feelings of fear to faith? Would you like to turn envy into compassion? The Bible shows us how David turned these negative emotions in his life into godly character qualities. By studying his life and choices we can make the same transformation in our own lives.

WISDOM: *Making Life Work*
Bill Hybels
Some people spend their lives relying on the abundance of information that's out there. But sometimes knowledge isn't enough. When we're stuck and don't know where to turn for answers, Proverbs offers practical advice and spiritual wisdom for real-life questions so that we might become people who think and act out of godly wisdom.

WITNESSING: *How to Give Away Your Faith*
Paul Little
If you want to talk about Jesus, but you're not sure what to say—or how to say it—this Bible study guide is for you. It will deepen your understanding of the essentials of faith and strengthen your confidence as you talk with others.